BASSET HOUNDS

FAVORITE DOG BREEDS

Dan Lopez

Norwood House Press

Cataloging-in-Publication Data

Names: Lopez, Dan.
Title: Basset hounds / Dan Lopez.
Description: Buffalo, NY : Norwood House Press, 2026. | Series: Favorite dog breeds| Includes glossary and index.
Identifiers: ISBN 9781978576629 (pbk.) | ISBN 9781978576636 (library bound) | ISBN 9781978576643 (ebook)
Subjects: LCSH: Basset hound--Juvenile literature.
Classification: LCC SF429.B2 L67 2026 | DDC 636.7536--dc23

Published in 2026 by
Norwood House Press
2544 Clinton Street
Buffalo, NY 14224

Designer: Rhea Magaro
Editor: Kim Thompson

Photo credits: Cover, p. 1 Rita_Kochmarjova, Giraphics/Shutterstock.com; p. 4 Wikipedia; p. 5 Billion Photos/Shutterstock.com; p. 6 Marcelino Pozo Ruiz/Shutterstock.com; p.8- 9 Eric Isselee/Shutterstock.com; p. 10 Paulina Modzelewska/Shutterstock.com; p. 11 Bukhta Yurii/Shutterstock.com; p. 13 Rawpixel.com/Shutterstock.com; p. 14 CHARLOTTE DINUNZIO/Shutterstock.com; p. 17 Jovica Varga/Shutterstock.com; p. 18 Kara Laws/Shutterstock.com; p. 19 Gabriela Tulian/Shutterstock.com; p. 21 tanya.asfir/Shutterstock.com

Printed in the United States of America

CPSIA compliance information: Batch #CWNHP26: For further information contact Norwood House Press at 1-800-237-9932.

TABLE OF CONTENTS

Meet the Basset Hound

Basset hounds are popular pets. Dogs of this **breed** are known for having big brown eyes, floppy **jowls**, and a powerful sense of smell.

Droopy is a famous cartoon basset hound.

What Do Basset Hounds Look Like?

Basset hounds are low to the ground. They have short legs and sausage-shaped bodies.

Adults can be 14 inches (36 centimeters) tall and weigh 60 pounds (27 kilograms).

A basset hound has a short, smooth **coat**.

Its fur can be black, tan, or white.

The basset hound has a loose, wrinkly face. Its floppy ears droop to the ground when it bends down to sniff.

The long ears stir up smells on the ground and direct them toward the dog's nose. Wrinkles on the face trap **scents** so the dog gets a good whiff.

Where Do Basset Hounds Come From?

Basset hounds have been around for hundreds of years. They were first raised in France as hunting dogs. The French word *basse* means “low.”

With their **keen** sense of smell, these dogs are excellent **trackers**. Their short, **stocky** bodies help them move through fields of thick brush. They can sniff out small animals such as birds, rabbits, and foxes.

Do Basset Hounds Make Good Pets?

Basset hounds are laid-back and easygoing. These gentle dogs are good **companions** for people of all ages.

Basset hounds can be stubborn. If they find an interesting smell, they are determined to follow it!

They do not make good **watchdogs**. They are friendly to everyone, even strangers.

What Do Basset Hounds Need?

Basset hounds like to play. They are very **social**. They need to be around people or other dogs, or they will get lonely.

Glossary

breed (breed): one type or kind of an animal

coat (koht): the hair or fur that covers an animal's body

companions (kuhm-PAN-yuhnz): friends, buddies, or partners

jowls (joulz): layers of loose skin that hang down around the throat or lower jaw

keen (keen): quick, sharp, sensitive, or highly developed

scents (sents): smells

social (SOH-shuhl): preferring to be around others instead of alone

stocky (STAH-kee): having a short, thick, and strong body

trackers (TRAK-urz): animals that are good at finding things by following trails left behind on the ground

watchdogs (WAHCH-dawgs): dogs kept to guard property

Thinking Questions

1. Describe a basset hound's face.
2. How does a basset hound's body help it smell and track?
3. Describe a basset hound's personality.
4. Why don't basset hounds make good watchdogs?
5. When can basset hounds be stubborn?

Index

About the Author

Dan Lopez is a writer who loves dogs! He has a German shepherd named Hans and an Irish setter named Tam. They love to go for walks in the woods together. Sometimes, they jump in the lake for a swim. Dan lives in Indiana with his wife and three kids.